Contents

Giant anteater

Can beetles bury the dead?

Burying beetles can bury animal bodies. They lay their eggs on the dead bodies of other animals. To make sure that their **larvae** get all of the rotting flesh for themselves, the parent beetles hide the body. They do this by digging away the soil underneath, so that the dead body is slowly lowered into the ground.

Burying beetles use their strong legs to dig away the soil underneath dead **mammals** and birds. Eventually the **carcasses** are buried underground, where the beetle larvae begin to feed on the flesh.

Wolf spider

Burying beetles

Dead bluetit

Scary Creatures OF THE SOIL

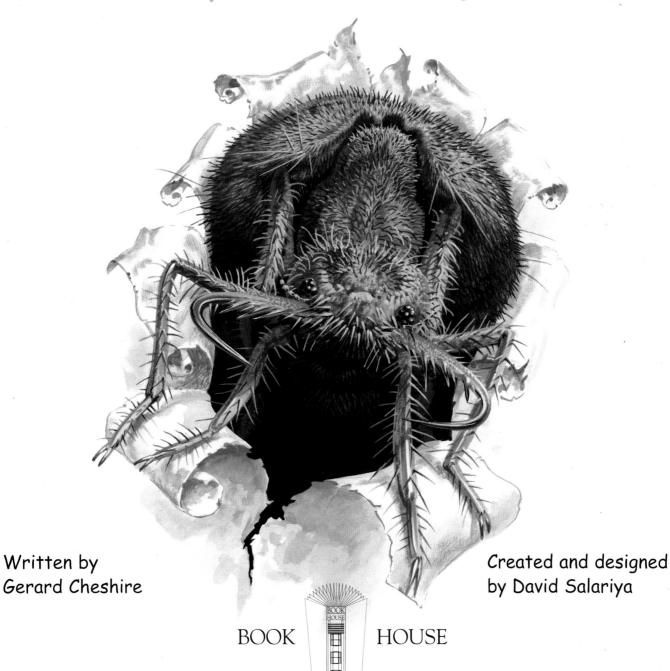

Written by
Gerard Cheshire

Created and designed
by David Salariya

BOOK HOUSE

Author:

Gerard Cheshire has written many books on natural history, and over the past twelve years has cultivated an excellent reputation as an author and editor. He now lives in Bath, England, with his wife and three sons.

David Salariya was born in Dundee, Scotland. He established The Salariya Book Company in 1989. He has illustrated a wide range of books and has created many new series for publishers in the UK and overseas. He lives in Brighton with his wife, illustrator Shirley Willis, and their son.

Editorial Assistants:
Rob Walker, Tanya Kant

Picture Research:
Mark Bergin, Carolyn Franklin

Photo Credits:

Dreamstime: 9, 16, 21, 22
Fotolia: 5, 6, 8, 25, 26
Jonathan Salariya: 18
iStockphoto: 10, 11, 12, 27
United States Department of Agriculture: 19

Visit our website at **www.salariya.com**
for *free* electronic versions of:
You Wouldn't Want to be an Egyptian Mummy!
You Wouldn't Want to be a Roman Gladiator!
Avoid Joining Shackleton's Polar Expedition!
Avoid Sailing on a 19th-Century Whaling Ship!

PAPER FROM
SUSTAINABLE
FORESTS

Published in Great Britain in 2009 by
Book House, an imprint of
The Salariya Book Company Ltd
25 Marlborough Place, Brighton BN1 1UB
A catalogue record for this book is available from the British Library.

HB ISBN: 978-1-906370-87-9
PB ISBN: 978-1-906370-88-6

Printed in China

Termite mound

Stag beetle

Mandible

Did You Know?

Some male beetles use their mandibles to fight each other for a **mate**. Sometimes a smaller male will mate with a female while bigger beetles are fighting over her.

Stag beetles look as though they can give painful bites, but their giant **mandibles** (jaws) are more like a deer's antlers and cannot do any harm.

Many beetles are black. This helps them to warm themselves by absorbing sunshine. The warmth gives them more energy to move about.

How do spiders ambush their prey?

All spiders are predators. They catch other animals and feed on their juices. Spiders catch their **prey** in a number of different ways. Most spiders use webs to catch their prey, but some spiders use different methods. Wolf spiders hunt their prey by running after it and grabbing it. Trapdoor spiders pounce on their prey from below. Woodlouse-eating spiders hunt at night and poison their prey.

A tangled web to trap insects

Orb spiders make neat spiralling webs to catch flying **insects**. Funnel-web spiders make funnel-shaped webs on the ground to catch walking insects. Some types of spider make tangled webs to catch landing insects.

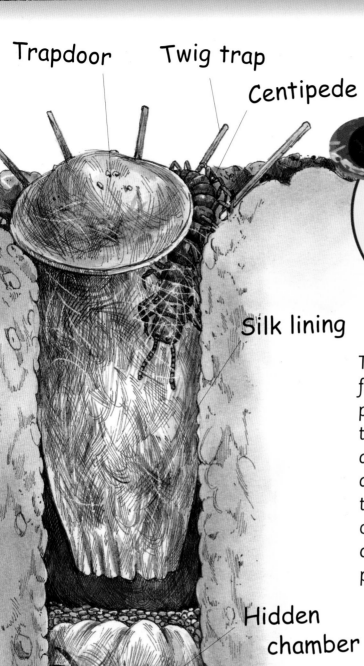

Trapdoor

Twig trap

Centipede

Silk lining

Hidden chamber

Trapdoor spider

Did You Know?

The trapdoor spider has sensitive hairs on its front two pairs of legs. These hairs detect vibrations made by passing animals. This is how the spider knows when its prey is near.

Trapdoor spiders use a trapdoor, made from silky strands of web, to catch prey and to hide from predators. The trapdoor is so well hidden that insects and other small animals walk over it, allowing the spider to grab them through the webbing. At the bottom of the spider's **burrow** is a hidden chamber. The spider hides here when predatory centipedes enter its burrow.

Trapdoor spider

Trapdoor spiders have special mouthparts that they use to dig their burrows.

7

What feeds poop to its babies?

Dung beetles, as their name implies, like to feed on animal dung (or poop). Some simply lay their eggs on dung, and their larvae burrow inside. Others, known as scarab beetles, role the dung into balls and then bury these as **larders** for their larvae. They bury the dung to protect their young from predators such as birds, and to hide the dung from other animals.

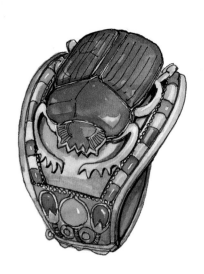

Egyptian ring

The ancient Egyptians worshipped scarab beetles. They believed that a giant scarab rolled the sun across the sky, just as beetles roll balls of dung. Khepri was the name of the Egyptian scarab god.

Scarab beetles have spiky front legs which they use to shape the balls of dung and to bury them, too.

Spiky front leg

Scarab beetle

Did You Know?

The name 'scarab' comes from the Latin word *scarabaeus*, which means 'beetle'.

Dung beetles

Usually the male rolls the dung ball with his hind legs, but sometimes male and female beetles work together.

How can owls nest where there are no trees?

When there are no trees for building nests, most birds just have to nest on the ground. This is dangerous, because it is easy for predators to find these nests and to eat the eggs and chicks inside them. The burrowing owl nests *under* the ground instead. It uses burrows that have been abandoned by rabbits or other animals – but the owl can use its feet to clear away loose soil and rocks.

The burrowing owl has long legs and large feet. It uses them to scrape loose soil and rocks out of old animal burrows before making its nest.

A pair of burrowing owls on the ground outside the entrance to their nest hole

Did You Know?

The cactus ferruginous pygmy owl lives in the Sonoran Desert of Arizona, USA. It nests in holes made by woodpeckers in the stems of cacti.

A burrowing owl sitting inside a hole dug by a prairie dog

What type of insect builds cities underground?

Some insects are described as **social insects**, because they live in vast **colonies** of hundreds or thousands that are almost like cities. Some social insects build their nests in the ground. Here they are safe from predators, and the temperature stays the same all year round. Ground-nesting social insects include ants, termites, bumblebees and some types of wasp.

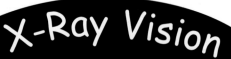

X-Ray Vision

Hold the next page up to the light and see what's inside a termite mound.

See what's inside

Termites

Termite nests are composed of many tunnels and chambers. The nests are made of mud which is a mixture of soil and the termites' own spit. When the mud dries out it is very hard and strong.

Termites are sometimes called 'white ants', but they are not closely related to real ants.

Termite mound

Inside a large
termite mound

Royal chamber

Queen

14

What's inside a termite mound?

Deep in the centre of the termite mound is the 'royal chamber' where the queen lives. Her job is to keep laying eggs so that there are always new termites to replace those that get eaten by predators. Although the queen is too large to move anywhere, she can produce anywhere from 2,000 to 30,000 eggs per day, depending on her **species**.

A large termite mound is rather like a castle. It has chimneys and vents to keep the nest cool during the heat of the day.

Most of the termites in a colony are either workers or soldiers. Workers do all of the nest maintenance and attend to the **queen**. Soldiers defend the nest against predators.

Male termites are called *kings*. They **fertilise** the queen so that her eggs can hatch into larvae.

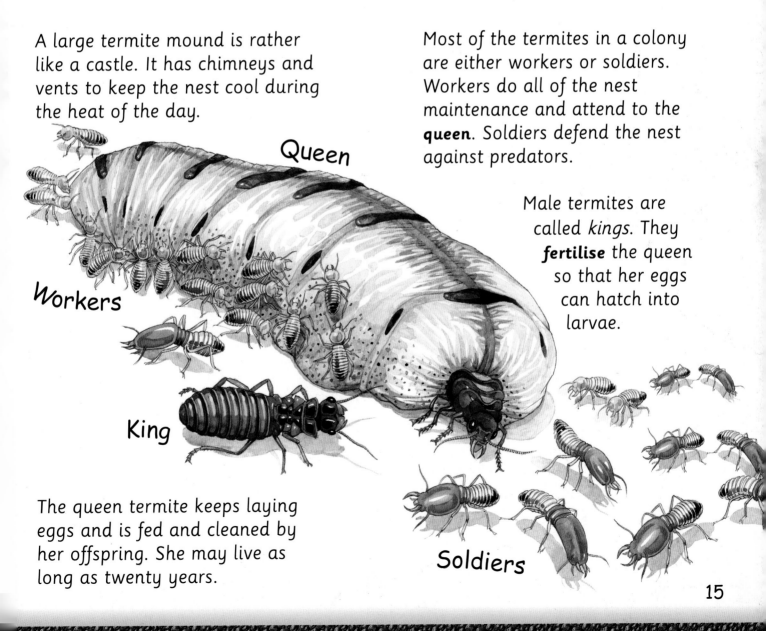

Queen

Workers

King

Soldiers

The queen termite keeps laying eggs and is fed and cleaned by her offspring. She may live as long as twenty years.

15

When are termites in trouble?

Termites make a good meal for animals that can break into their nests. One expert termite eater is the giant anteater. It has enormous claws on its front feet that can rip holes in a termite mound. It also has a long snout, which it pokes inside the nest to feed on the termites. It uses its long, sticky tongue to lap up the insects in their thousands.

Giant anteater

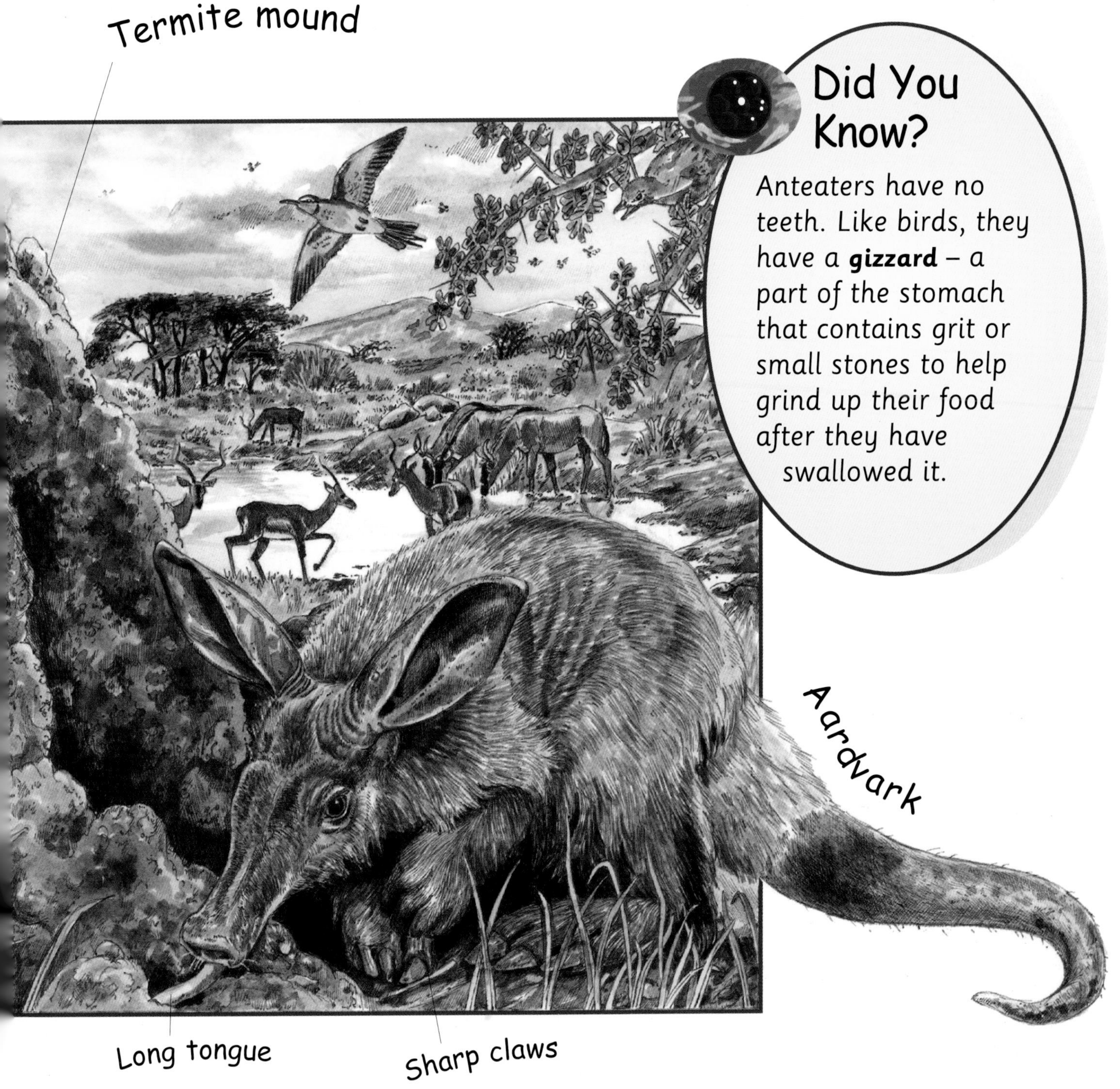

Termite mound

Aardvark

Long tongue

Sharp claws

Aardvarks emerge from their underground burrows in the late afternoon to **forage** for ants or termites. They scoop up termites with their 30-cm-long tongue.

Other termite-eaters include armadillos, pangolins and echidnas. Like anteaters, they all have large claws to break into nests and long snouts to eat termites.

When the predators have eaten their fill, the termites repair their nest.

Worms

Worms eat rotted carcasses buried in the ground. As carcasses **decompose**, their **nutrients** are released into the soil and worms **recycle** them.

Why are worms good for soil?

Earthworms are very important for the soil. They create a network of tunnels, which keep the soil well drained and **ventilated**. This helps plants to grow well. Worms also eat the pieces of animals and plants that have rotted into the soil. Their own faeces (poop) then enriches the soil, making it even better for plants.

What is a nematode worm?

Nematode worms are smaller than earthworms and their bodies are not divided into segments (ring-like sections). The elegant nematode worm is only 1mm long but plays a very important role in the decomposition and recycling of nutrients.

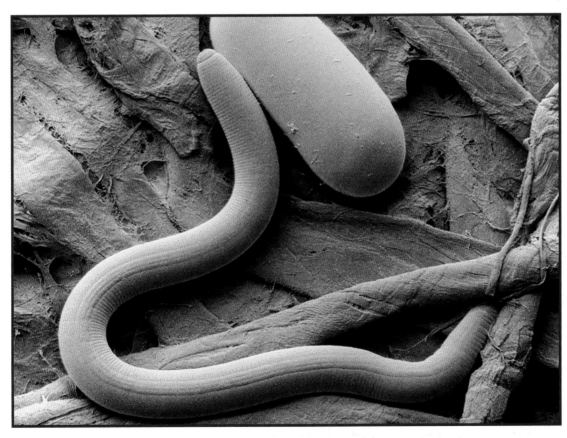

Nematode worm and its egg, seen through a microscope

Can lions live in the ground?

Of course, real lions don't live underground, but one insect is so fearsome that it is named after a lion! The adult antlion is a flying insect rather like a dragonfly, but its larva is a predator of ants. Another insect named after a big cat is the tiger beetle (see pages 26–27).

Did You Know?

Antlions can be found in warm habitats all over the world. They live in sandy, shaded areas such as riverbanks, dry forests, and even building sites.

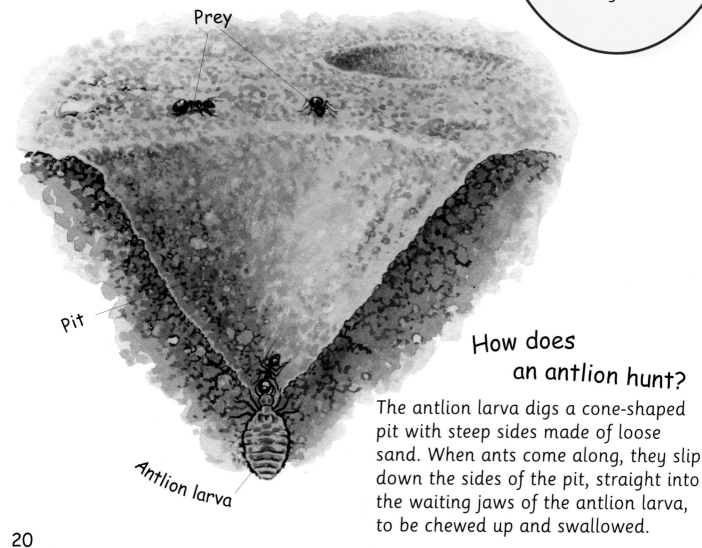

Prey

Pit

Antlion larva

How does an antlion hunt?

The antlion larva digs a cone-shaped pit with steep sides made of loose sand. When ants come along, they slip down the sides of the pit, straight into the waiting jaws of the antlion larva, to be chewed up and swallowed.

To humans, an antlion larva is very small and harmless, but to an ant it is a giant monster.

Antlion larva

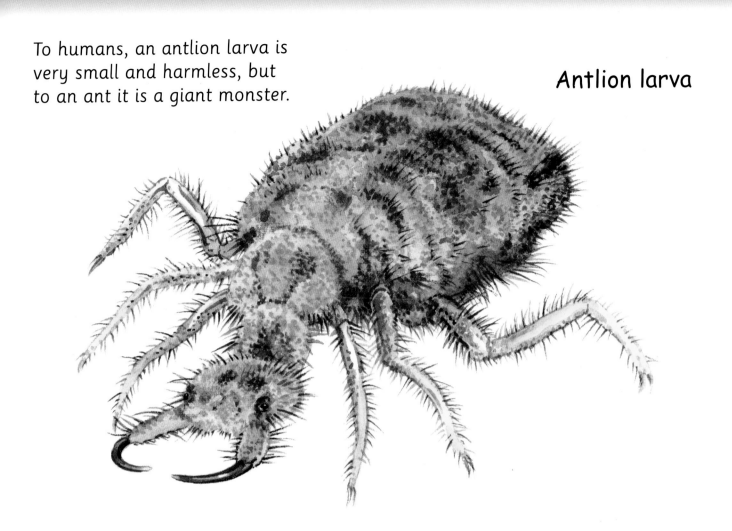

How does a larva become an adult?

When a larva is fully grown, it goes through a process called **metamorphosis** which turns it into a flying adult. It then goes off to find a mate.

Adult antlion

Are there tiny tigers?

Tiger beetles and their larvae are ferocious predators of other insects and **invertebrates**. The tiger beetle larva ambushes its prey by hiding in the ground and then pouncing on creatures that come too close. The adult beetle is very quick and agile. Its large, forward-facing eyes help it to spot its victims.

Did You Know?

If a tiger beetle were the same size as a human, it could run ten times faster than the fastest sprinter.

Tiger beetle

The tiger beetle uses its powerful jaws to grab and pierce its prey.
Then it releases fluid that turns the prey into mush.

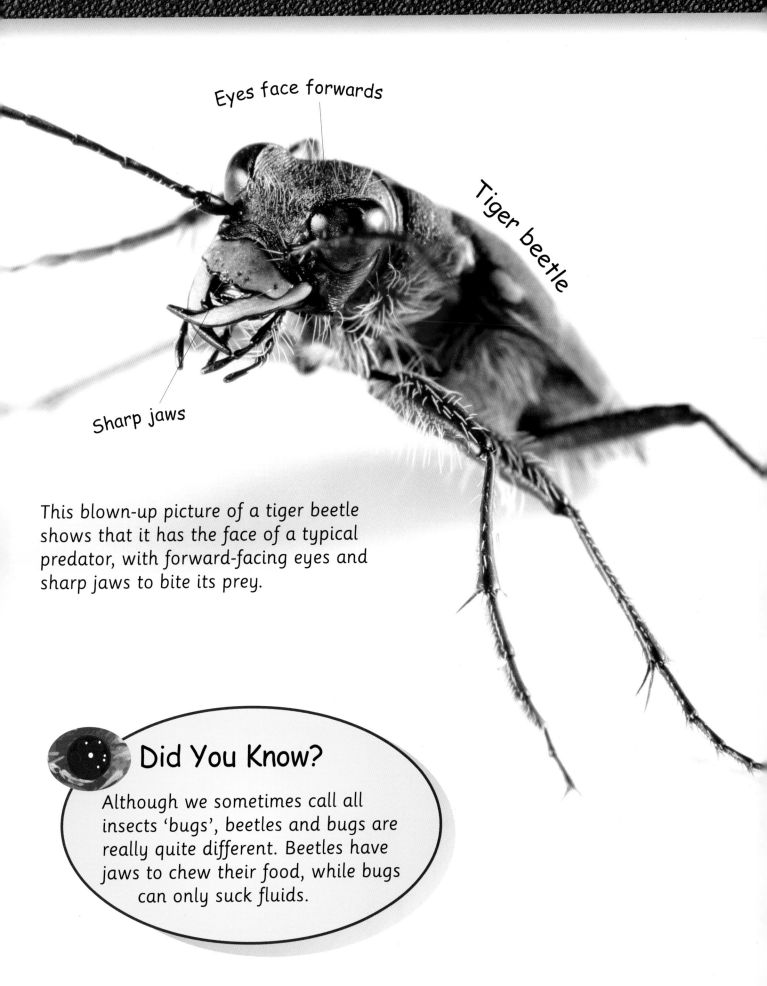

Eyes face forwards

Tiger beetle

Sharp jaws

This blown-up picture of a tiger beetle shows that it has the face of a typical predator, with forward-facing eyes and sharp jaws to bite its prey.

Did You Know?

Although we sometimes call all insects 'bugs', beetles and bugs are really quite different. Beetles have jaws to chew their food, while bugs can only suck fluids.

What lives in a hole?

There are many larger animals that live in holes in the ground. They include mammals, birds and **reptiles**. Living below ground provides safety from predators and protection from the weather. Some animals also find their food under the ground.

X-Ray Vision

Hold the page opposite up to the light to see why these rabbits are hiding in their burrow.

See what's inside

Prairie dogs

Prairie dogs are not dogs, but **rodents** rather like large hamsters. They live in colonies and dig networks of tunnels.

Moles live and feed underground, eating worms and other invertebrates that they come across.

Mole

Weasel

How safe is a burrow?

Predators such as stoats, weasels, polecats, ferrets, mink and snakes have long, narrow bodies. They can easily enter the tunnels of animals that live underground.
For this reason, many burrowing animals build escape tunnels so that they can get away if predators come looking for them.

Rattlesnake

Snakes are dangerous predators for animals below ground. They can slip down tunnels in silence and quickly bite their prey before it has time to escape.

Weasel

A weasel's body is no wider than its head. If it can get its head inside a tunnel, it knows that its body will fit too.

Did You Know?

Rattlesnakes bite their prey and then follow the victim's scent trail until the poison kills it. Then they can easily swallow it.

Where do these scary creatures live?

Burrowing animals are found in almost every part of the world. This map shows where some of them live.

North America

South America

Burrowing owl

The burrowing owl comes from desert areas in North and South America, where there are no trees in which to nest.

Prairie dog

Prairie dogs, as their name suggests, come from the prairies (grasslands) of North America.

Rattlesnake

Rattlesnakes come from arid, dry regions in the Americas.

Giant anteater

Giant anteaters live in regions of South America where termites build their mounds.

Antlion larva

Antlions live in sandy places, where their larvae can build cone-shaped pits to trap ants.

Mole

Moles come from **temperate** places where the soil is easy to tunnel through, with plenty of worms.

Asia

Europe

Africa

Australasia

Trapdoor spider

Trapdoor spiders are common in parts of Asia and Australasia where it is warm and fairly dry.

Antarctica

Termite

Termites live in warm places around the world, including Africa, Asia, the Americas and Australia.

Scarab beetle

The scarab beetle was once worshipped in Egypt; it can be found all over the world.

Soil facts

There are around 70,000 different types of soil in the United States alone.

Soil is formed by natural processes such as the wearing away of rocks by wind and rain. It takes hundreds of years for even a centimetre of soil to be formed in this way.

Up to one million earthworms can live in just one acre (0.4 hectare) of soil.

If an earthworm is cut or torn in two by a predator, the worm can sometimes regrow the missing end and keep on living as normal. But it's not true that both ends can grow to make two worms.

Termite mounds in the deserts of Australia have measured over 13 metres high and 30 metres in circumference.

Mole mounds – the mounds of soil that moles leave behind as they dig – can be up to 60 cm tall.

Trapdoor spiders can live for up to 20 years. They usually stay in the same burrow, widening it to fit them as they grow.

Weasels are predators of many burrowing animals, such as rabbits. But weasels themselves fall prey to bigger animals such as foxes, hawks and cats. Only about one weasel out of 80 lives to over two years of age.

A burying beetle can completely bury a small animal carcass in around 8 hours.

Giant anteaters are threatened by humans in two ways. They are hunted for trophies, and their Central and South American **habitats** are being destroyed by human development.

European rabbits are very social animals and live in groups of around 20. They live in burrow systems known as 'warrens'.

The larva of the American cicada can remain hidden in the soil for 17 years before developing into an adult.

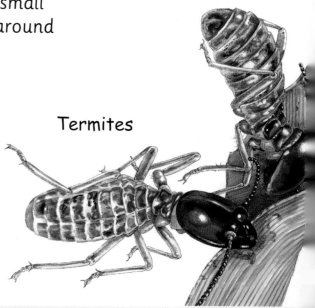

Termites

Glossary

burrow (noun) A hole that an animal lives in.

carcass A dead body.

colony A large group of the same type of animal that lives together.

decompose To rot and break down into separate parts.

fertilisation What happens when egg and sperm are combined to produce offspring.

forage To go out looking for food.

gizzard A part of the stomach, in birds and some other animals, in which food is ground down by stones or grit.

habitat The place where an animal lives naturally.

insect An invertebrate with six legs and a body made of three parts: head, thorax and abdomen.

invertebrate An animal with no backbone.

larder A place used for storing or hiding food.

larva (plural **larvae**) The young of an animal, such as an insect, that will change into a different form when it becomes an adult.

mammal A warm-blooded animal with body hair or fur, that feeds its young on mother's milk.

mandibles Jaws or mouthparts, especially those of an insect.

mate (noun) A partner of the opposite sex; (verb) to join together to make offspring.

metamorphosis The process by which insects change from larvae into adults.

nutrients The food or chemicals that a living thing needs in order to live and grow.

predator An animal that kills and eats other animals.

prey An animal that is killed and eaten by a predator.

queen A female insect that lays eggs. In a colony of social insects there is usually only one queen.

recycle To make something new (such as new animals) out of something old (such as the nutrients in a dead animal).

reptile A cold-blooded animal with scales.

rodent A mammal with gnawing teeth, such as a mouse or rat.

social insects Insects that live together in large colonies.

temperate Neither very hot nor very cold.

ventilated Open to a current of fresh air.

Index

Mole